Low Carb Casseroles:

25 Super Delicious Low Carb Casseroles for Weight Loss

Table of content

Introduction

Low Carb Casseroles are meals which are eaten to reduce weight by many people. If you are trying to lose weight then do not go on dieting plan but instead exercise and have healthy food which contains all the necessary nutrients you need. It is obvious that every ingredient cannot be eaten separately due to which there are delicious recipes for you to try. Casseroles do not have anything oily in them because they are baked and cooked under the same heat.

They are surely the perfect diet plan which you can use during the process of losing weight. You can make a casserole and keep it for 2-3 days to eat it on and off. This will be included in your weight loss plan. They are low in carbs and fat which help you get lean. No matter you like chicken, beef, vegetable or any other thing made of casserole, they are amazing to try. There are proteins in the meat whether it is white meat or red meat. Along with that, vegetables provide you the nutrients which you may miss while working out daily so gain them back but in a healthy way.

Chapter 1 – Chicken Casserole Recipes

1.   ***Chicken Veg. Casserole***

Ingredients:

-   Chicken (boneless)
-   Oil (according to your choice)
-   Carrots (2)
-   Onion (2)
-   Seasoning (Cajun)
-   Juice (Orange ¼ cup)
-   Peas (as needed)
-   Chicken broth
-   Dill (chopped)
-   Parsley

Recipe:

First of all, put the chicken in to a pot and boil the water in it. Once it is boiled, keep it aside. On the other hand, turn on the oven to 375 degrees F. Let it get warm and heat the stove, add oil as needed to the pan and add onion and carrots. Cook them until they look soft and sprinkle the seasoning of Cajun on it. Let it stay there of about 10-15 minutes.

Cook the vegetables and stir it for about 5 minutes. Add the orange juice and the broth until it boils. Add the peas and parsley and once they are cooked, pour in the buttermilk. Transfer everything to a baking pan and then place chicken on it. Let it stay in oven for about 10-15 minutes. Now, take it out and it is ready to eat!

Health Benefits:

25g Protein

13g Fat

340 Calories

30g Carbs

2. *Chi-Broccoli Casserole*

Ingredients:

- Butter (any)
- Mayonnaise (half can)
- Mushroom soup (any brand)
- Salt and pepper according to taste

- Onion as needed
- Chicken (cooked and mashed)
- Broccoli (chopped)

Recipe:

Spread butter on the baking dish so that it stays moist for the ingredients to stay on it. Now, heat the oven to 375 degrees Fahrenheit. While it warms up, take a bowl and stir the cream, soup and the mayonnaise together. Add salt and pepper as desired. Add the onions in it which should be chopped with the shredded cheese. Now cover the chicken as well as the broccoli in all this mixture.

Now shift all the mixture including the chicken into the baking dish and put it in the oven for about 5-6 minutes. Now as it gets cooked, take it out and season it so that it melts in between the hot chi-broccoli casserole which you will enjoy eating.

Healthy Benefits:
3g carbs per serving
Protein 21 g
Fat 6 g
Sodium 80 mg

3.   ***Chicken Mushroom Casserole***

Ingredients:
- Oil as needed
- Onion (1)
- Mushrooms (as required)
- Garlic (cloves)
- Spinach as needed
- Parsley
- Milk (2-3 cups)
- Salt and pepper to taste
- Chicken
- Almonds for seasoning

Recipe:

At first, you need to warm up the oven up to 375 degree F. Now oil the baking dish in which you are going to place the casserole. On other side, take the pan and heat it over low heat. Fry the onions which are sliced and cook them for about 6-7 minutes. Add mushrooms and let them cook as well.

Now add garlic and let it cook for about a minute. Take a bowl and transfer all of it in it. In the same pan, you need to pour milk in it as desired. As the milk warms up, take it off the heat. If you want, you can add salt and pepper as well. Now the cheese melts and you will see how smooth and soft the sauce is.

Take chicken and make it boneless. Or if you have it boneless before then it is perfect. Add the chicken into the cheese mixture and coat it all. Now, put it all into the baking dish and let it cook in oven for about 5-7 minutes. You will sense a smell that it has been cooked, now take it out and shred the almonds on it as seasoning or any other seasoning you like.

Health Benefits:
Calories 22
Total Fat 0.3 g
Carbohydrate 3.3 g

4.   *The Nacho Casserole*

Ingredients:

-    Chicken breast (as needed)

- Tomatoes
- Carrots
- Garlic (Cloves)
- Red Chili powder
- Cheese (Feta preferable) (low fat)
- Cilantro
- Sauce (any you like)

Recipe:

This is a quick and easy to make recipe where you have to heat the oven first at 400 degrees F. Take the baking dish and spray it over with the cooking spray. Take the bowl and mix all the ingredients along with chicken breast piece.

Take the bowl which you have sprayed and add all the mixture in it. Bake it for about 20-25 minutes in the oven and when it is done and top it up with your favorite seasoning of mint or parsley. And note, if you want you can add any kind of sauce on it.

Healthy Benefits:
Calories 23
Carbohydrate 3.7 g
Fat 0.5 g
Protein 27 g

5.   *Spicy Chicken filled Casserole*

Ingredients:

- Salsa (the main ingredient so do not miss this)
- Tomato sauce as needed
- Chipotle sauce
- Chicken chopped
- Salt and pepper as needed
- Cheese Shredded (low fat)
- Cilantro as needed

Recipe:

Heat up the oven to 400 degree F. Oil the baking dish and then add the salsa and sauces together. Pour them in separate bowl and then add the chicken into it.

Add the chicken. Put a layer of shredded cheese on chicken and cilantro as well. Do this again by making the same layer over the shredded cheese. This is how you will make the serving thicker and delicious.

Now when you are done with all the dressings, take the entire baking dish and bake it for about 20-25 minutes. Make sure to keep on checking it until it cooks properly. Once it is cooked, take it out carefully and serve it in pieces by cutting it.

13

Health Benefits:

Protein 27g

Vitamin A 3%

Iron 7%

Chapter 2 – Vegetable Casseroles

6. *The Squashy Casserole*

Ingredients:

- Oil as needed, if you have a spray that would be better.
- Squash
- Onions (2)
- Cheese (shredded) (low fat)
- Salt and pepper as needed
- Pimientos (diced considered)
- Sauce (any)
- Basil
- Garlic (cloves)

Recipe:

Heat up the oven up to 350 degree F. Cover the baking dish with the oil or if you have spray then that would make it convenient for you. The whole dish should be mildly moist with the oil.

Take a pot and cook all the main ingredients in it such as onion, squash and pimientos. Make sure to cook the vegetables since you are going to keep it all in the oven to bake it at the end. Now when the vegetables are boiled, take them out of water. Add all the ingredients together and then add the salt and pepper to taste.

Take all the mixture and pour it all in the casserole baking dish. Now cook it for about 40 minutes in the oven. Keep a track of time and when it is cooked, take it out and let it cool a bit then it is ready to eat.

Health Benefits:

Fat 0.3 g
Protein 1.2 g
Calories 17
Carbohydrate 3.1 g

7.   *The Delicious Pepper Casseroles*

Ingredients:
- Peppers (3 different kinds)
- Sour Cream (low fat)
- Milk (skimmed or low fat)
- Salsa
- Cheese (low fat)

- Cilantro leaves
- Onions (cut properly in round shape)

Recipe:

Turn on the broiler of the oven and cook the peppers in it for about 10-15 minutes so that they are soft enough to be chewed. Take them out and cover them in foil. Now turn on the oven and heat it to 350 degree F. Until it warms up, take a bowl and add the sour cream and milk together. Mix it well so it takes a shape of a thick cream.

Now put the layer of the cream and milk mixture. Repeat the layers two three times more in order to make it thick.

Now, bake it for about 50 minutes in the oven and keep the heat consistent. Do not check it again and again since it cooks in the warmth of the oven. As you see the top of the meal getting brownish then it is time to take it out before it burns. You can add the cheese before baking or after it, however you like it. Spread the onions and cilantro on it to serve the dish and enjoy it.

Health Benefits:
Carbohydrates 63 g
Fat 1.2 g
Protein 21 g

8.   *The Artichokes Casseroles*

Ingredients:

- Artichokes (peeled)
- Fennel
- Cream (low fat)
- Garlic (cloves)
- Nutmeg
- Salt and pepper as desired

Recipe:

Turn on the oven and heat it to 350 degree F. until it warms up, take the pot on the other side and add all the ingredients in it. Bring it to boil. Make sure they are cooked. Now reduce the heat and let them cook under the heat.

Take a baking dish and spray it with the cooking oil, add the mixture in the baking dish and cover it with the breadcrumbs. Put it in the oven for about 40 minutes and it will be ready to eat.

Health Benefits:

Fat 0.2 g
Carbohydrate 11 g
Protein 3.3 g

9.   *The Cauliflower Casserole*

Ingredients:

- Pumpkin seeds
- Butter
- Cauliflower
- Cheese (low fat)

- Mustard seeds
- Salt and pepper as taste
- Garlic (cloves)
- Half and half cream (half cup)

Recipe:

First you have to get all the vegetables together in order to bake them. Heat up the oven up to 400 degree F. Spray the baking dish so that the ingredients do not stick to it and it is easy to take it out as well after baking. Now mix all the ingredients together from the first ingredient to the end except cauliflower. You have to create layers with layering the cauliflower on the mixture. Repeat the layers 2-3 times. Now when all the mixture is ready, cook it in oven for about 30-35 minutes.

After baking you have to do the seasoning. Now when you are done, you will see the brownish toppings, so it is ready to eat!

Healthy Benefits:

Calories 25

Carbohydrate 5 g

Protein 1.9 g

10. *The Favorite Spinach Casserole*

Ingredients:

- Milk (low fat)
- Cream (low fat)
- Garlic (cloves)
- Bay leaf
- Salt as desired
- Bacon (slices)
- Spinach leaves
- Butter as needed
- Onions
- Cheese (low fat)
- Lemon juice
- Pepper as needed (grounded)

Recipe:

Get a pan and cook the milk, cream and the bay leaf in it. On the other side, turn on the oven to 350 degrees F. Now when it has boiled, take out the milk and cream mixture aside for a while.

You have to cook the bacon slices until they look crispy. Also, in the same pan, cook the spinach lightly but make sure it does not mash in between. Add salt and pepper as of your taste. When it is down, take it out in the bowl and keep it aside to cool.

Now in the same pan, add butter and melt it. Cook the onions and garlic until they look tender to you. Put cheese and the lemon juice and stir it all. Now you have three things which are separate. You need to add all this into the baking dish and cook in the oven for about 30-40 minutes. If you wish, you can add more cheese on top of the baking dish to make it delicious. Once cooked, let it cool for 10 minutes then it is ready to serve.

Health Benefit:
Calories 23
Carbohydrate 3.6 g
Protein 2.9 g

Chapter 3 – Beef and Mutton Casseroles

11.   *Beef Casserole with Onions*

Ingredients:

- Butter
- Onions (3)
- Garlic (chopped)
- Bay Leaf (1)
- Thyme
- Mushrooms
- Oil as needed
- Steak (cut into dices)
- Salt and pepper to taste
- Beef broth
- Wine (red)
- Sauce
- Sour Cream (low fat)
- Parsley

Recipe:

Take out the pan and add the butter to melt in it. Now add the chopped onions, garlic and bay leaf in it to cook. Add salt and pepper as desired. Cook this until you see them light brown, now add the thyme also at the end, and cook it for 5 more minutes. Now, put the mushrooms and keep the heat low.

After it is cooked, take it out in a bowl and keep it separate. Now make the sauces by getting them all together and cook them for about 5 minutes. Once you are done with that, take the sour cream and mix it all together. Take the beef mixture and wash it with water. Then keep it on a low heat with the red wine in it because that helps the beef cook faster. Once it is cooked, take it off and keep it separate. Melt the cheese and spread it over the cooked beef. Mix everything together and season it with parsley. Serve it hot with buns.

Health Benefits:

Protein 26 g

Carbohydrate 0 g

Potassium 318 mg

Sodium 72 mg

12.   *Meaty Casserole*

Ingredients:
- Meatballs
- Sauce
- Cheese (low fat)
- Seasoning(any you like)

Recipe:

You can buy the frozen meatballs from the market or you can also cook them yourself. If you are someone who does not like to spend more time in kitchen then catch a pack of meatballs from the store and get started. Turn on the oven to 350 degrees F and put the meatballs to cook in the oven heat. Keep it inside for about 5 minutes. Take it out and then pour the sauces as desired. Add the cheese on the meatballs by covering it.

Bake it for about 20 minutes and it is ready to it. Do the seasoning whichever you like according to your taste.

Health Benefits:

Protein 21 g

Carbohydrate 8 g

Potassium 180 mg

Sodium 550 mg

Fat 9 g

13. *Ground Beef Casserole*
Ingredients:

- Beef
- Onion (chopped)
- Salt and pepper to taste
- Water (half cup)
- Sauce (tomato)
- Cheese (low fat)
- Mixed vegetables
- Biscuits (any)
- Butter
- Oregano

Recipe:

Heat the oven to 375 degrees F. Take out a baking dish and spray it with oil so that the ingredients do not stick to it. Take a pan and cook the beef in it so that it is not raw. When you see it cooking half way then add the onions in it which should be chopped. You can season it with salt and pepper if you want. Add the water and then add the sauce in the same pan. Let it cook for a bit until you feel that it is ready.

Now spread the entire mixture as a layer in the baking dish and cover it with cheese which should be shredded. Add the vegetables accordingly by covering the entire dish as a layer and then add cheese on it again.

Adding the crunch to it, take the biscuits and crush them. Spread them over the dish and put it oven for about 25 minutes to cook. Also when it is half way cooked, add the oregano on top of it and let it cook for another 10 minutes. You will be ready with the dish to eat at the lunch/dinner.

Health benefits:

Protein 14 g

Potassium 218 mg

Sodium 67 mg

14. *The Cheesy Beef Casserole*

Ingredients:

- Butter
- Onion (chopped)
- Garlic (cloves)
- Mushroom
- Cream (low fat)
- Chicken
- Pepper and Salt as taste
- Beef (grounded)
- Carrots
- Cheese (slices) (low fat)

Recipe:

Heat the pan on the light heat and then melt the butter in it. Add the onion and garlic and cook it. Later on add mushrooms to it and wait until it is cooked light brownish. Cook for about a minute and then add cream and broth in it. Making it thick paste. When you think it is ready, then take it off the heat.

On the other hand, turn on the oven to 350 degrees F and spray it the oil in it. Now add the cream which you cooked, spread the beef. Make sure to combine it all in the baking dish and place it in the oven. In the middle, take it out and add cheese on it. After that cook for 10 more minutes and take it out to eat it.

Health Benefits:

Protein 18 g

Potassium 213 mg

Sodium 48mg

15.   *The Beef Noodle Casserole*

Ingredients:

- Pasta
- Beef (grounded)
- Sauce
- Garlic
- Salt and pepper as needed
- Sour Cream (low fat)

- Cheese (shredded) (low fat)
- Onions (green)

Recipe:

Turn on the oven to the heat of 350 Degree F. keep the baking dish prepared with the oil on it lightly spread. You should have pasta cooked on the other hand so that it is ready to be added to the dish. Now, cook beef in the pan so that it is fully ready when you are ready to put it in oven. Stir it and add the sauces in it as well as salt and pepper. Cook it for about 10 minutes and then let it cool.

In another bowl, add the cream and the cheese together making it a thick paste. Now combine everything in the dish and at the end pour the cream thick paste on it. Place it in the oven for about 30 minutes and you will love it once it is ready to eat!

Health benefits:

Protein 19 g
Potassium 214 mg
Sodium 49 mg

Chapter 4 – Ham Casseroles with Delicious Flavors

16.   *Ham Casserole*

Ingredients:
- Noodles
- Ham
- Cheese (1 cup) (low fat)
- Cream (low fat)
- Milk (Low-Fat)
- Butter (1 teaspoon)

Recipe:

Cook the ham as they are tender. Now keep the ham in the dish with the butter on it. Mix the ham and cheese together and spread it over the casserole dish. Mix the milk and the soup of ham and create its layer on top of the mixture. Put it in oven at the heat of 375 degree F for about 30-40 minutes and it will be ready to enjoy.

Health benefits:

Protein 31 g
Fat 7 g
Carbohydrate 1.4g

17. Hash Brown Casserole with Ham

Ingredients:
- Cheese (low fat)
- Soup
- Cream (low fat)
- Onions (3)
- Ham (should be diced)
- Cajun for seasoning
- Butter as needed
- Salt and pepper as needed

Recipe:

This is the easiest recipe of all, all you need to do is to mix all the ingredients in the bowl and then place them in a casserole dish with mixing the ham in it. The ham should be cooked before in order for it to be tender. Place the dish in the oven for about 30 minutes and you will be done with cooking the delicious meal.

Health Benefit:

Protein 21 g
Potassium 190mg
Sodium 89 mg

18. Ham and cheese casserole

Ingredients:
- Onions

- Butter as needed
- Milk (half cup) (low fat)
- Sauce
- Yellow mustard
- Salt and pepper as needed
- Cheese (low fat)
- Ham, should be cooked

Recipe:

In a pan, cook the onion in the butter. Make sure that they are dried when you have cooked them. Place them in a separate plate. Make the white sauce now and blend it thoroughly. Add the salt and pepper as desired. Mix it well until it turns thick.

Now you need to get everything in the dish by creating layers. Cover the dish with the ham and then cheese over it. Then place the ham on it with cheese above it. Then cover it again with cheese layer. Bake this for 20 minutes in the oven for 350 degree F and it will be ready to serve.

Health Benefit:
Protein 21 g
Fat 6 g
Carbohydrate 1.5 g

19. *Ham Celery Casserole*

Ingredients:

- Butter
- Celery
- Onions
- Cooked Ham
- Half and Half cream
- Salt and pepper as needed
- Nutmeg
- Cheese (low fat)

Recipe:

Turn on the oven to heat it at 350 degree F. butter the casserole dish. Take a pan and then add celery until it is tender. Further, add the onions and the ham which should be cooked before however you like it to be cooked. Mix it all well and then add the salt and pepper to taste. Also add nutmeg at the end. Mix it gently. Take it all out in a bowl and then melt the cheese in the pan for the dressing.

Now put everything in the casserole dish by placing the ham first and then the mixture. Over it, pour the melted cheese. Let it cook for about 30 minutes and when it turns light brown color, take it out and eat it with your friends or family.

Health benefit:

Protein 19 g

Fat 8 g

Carbohydrate 1.5 g

20. Ham Casserole with Vegetables

Ingredients:

- Carrots
- Green pepper
- Ham Diced (cooked)
- Onion
- Celery
- Half and half cream (low fat)
- Salt and pepper to add taste
- Parsley
- Cheese (low fat)

Recipe:

Cover the dish with butter and turn on the oven to 325 degree F. Heat the flame and add butter in the pan. As it gets warm, add onion and make sure they turn soft. Add the green pepper as well as the carrots in it to be cooked. Now you can add the salt and pepper to taste as well. Cut the carrots in to slices and then make sure to cook them separately as well.

Pour all this to the baking dish and the dress it with the cheese. Cook it in the oven for about 45 minutes and check in between if the cheese is being turned brown. You will get to know when it is cooked by its delicious smell. Once cooked, it is ready to be served hot.

Health benefit:
Protein 22 g
Fat 5 g
Carbohydrate 1.9 g

Chapter 5 – Italian and Mexican Casseroles

21. *The Fajita Casserole*

Ingredients:
- Sauce (tomato or any other)
- Chicken breast
- Onions
- Fajita for seasoning
- Cheese (low fat)

Recipe:

Heat the oven to 375 degrees F and take out the baking dish. Now here is a certain order which you need to follow in order to make perfect fajita casserole. Put the chicken at the bottom. Take a bowl and mix all and sauce together. Put a layer of it at the top. Now in the same bowl, take the chicken and the fajita, mix it well and put that layer on the dish. Cover it with cheese. Bake for about 30 minutes and cook it until you see the brown topping of cheese.

Health Benefit:
Protein 21 g
Fat 4 g
Carbohydrate 1.6 g

22. *Hot Jalapeno Casserole*

Ingredients:

- Spinach
- Butter
- Onion (chopped)
- Jalapeno (chopped or normal sized)
- Sour cream (low fat)
- Cumin seeds
- Cheese (low fat)
- Chicken (small pieces or sliced)

Recipe:

Wash the spinach first and then let it dry. Heat the oven to 350 degrees F and let it get warm. On the other hand, take a pan and put butter in it to melt. Now add all the main ingredients to be cooked as well as the cream to make it a thick paste. Add the cumin also accordingly.

Now put it all in the baking dish by layering on the top the chicken on it. Repeat the layers and bake it in the oven for about 45 minutes. Make sure that the cheese is melt before you take it out.

Health benefits:

Protein 21 g

Fat 5 g

Carbohydrate 1.3 g

23.   *Cheese Beef Bell Casserole*

Ingredients:

- Beef
- Onion
- Garlic powder
- Tomato sauce
- Sour cream (low fat)
- Cheese (any you want) (low fat)

Recipe:

Heat the oven to 350 degree F. Take a pan and cook the beef in it. You always have to cook the beef or chicken before baking so that you get good results once the meal is fully cooked. Add onion and garlic powder into the beef mixture and put it aside when done.

Now mix the cream and the cheese to make it thick paste. After you are done with it, take the baking dish and pour both of these mixtures in it. Cover it with cheese. Put it in oven and cook it for about 20 minutes. After cooked, serve hot.

Health benefit:

Protein 19 g

Fat 8 g

Carbohydrate 1.8g

Sodium 82 mg

24.   The Beefy Tamale Casserole

Ingredients:

- Grounded beef
- Onion (chopped)
- Tomatoes
- Red chili powder
- Salt and pepper according to taste
- Milk (3 cups) (low fat)
- Olives (black)
- Cheese (low fat)

Recipe:

Heat the oven to 350 degree F and take out the pan. You have to make things separate in order to combine them at the end to bake. Cook the beef and add onions to it, add the tomatoes and mix it well. Make sure that the beef is cooked well otherwise it will ruin the taste of the meal.

On the other side, cook the milk and mix it well so it gets thick. Now, place everything in the dish and pour the thick paste on it. Bake it for about 30 minutes and you delicious meal will be ready.

Health benefit:

Protein 22 g

Fat 6 g

Carbohydrate 1.7g

Sodium 70 mg

25. *Chicken Cream Casserole (low fat)*

Ingredients:

- Chicken (cooked)
- Tomatoes
- Cream (low fat)
- Cheese (low fat)

Recipe:

Heat the oven to 350 degrees F. Take a bowl and mix all the ingredients well with each other. That will be added at the end. Put the dish in the oven and cook it for about 20 minutes. When done, take it out and as a layer add more cheese. It adds the softness taste to the meal. Enjoy the delicious chicken meal!

Health benefits:

Protein 21 g

Fat 4 g

Carbohydrate 1.5g

Sodium 90 mg

Conclusion

These are easy recipes which you can try at home with the basic ingredients which mostly everyone has in their home. If you are someone who does not like to spend much time in the kitchen then these are the best casseroles recipes for you to try. You will enjoy making them and at the end when you get best results you would love to try every new recipe. There is no frying included in any of the recipes, you simply have to cook some of the ingredients and mostly every recipe involves the baking part which makes it healthy for you.

There are all kinds of recipes whether you love chicken, vegetable, ham or beef. All different recipes have been mentioned in this eBook for you to learn and know how easy they are to make. They do not consume much of your time and you will be able to have a good lunch with your buddies. Choose your best one and make it now in order to get the real taste of it. They are amazing and even by reading, it makes one hungry. The delicious recipes are just one step away, you just need to get into the kitchen.

All the recipes take less than 10 minutes to assemble them together and then bake them until it cooks and ready to eat! Catch the best recipes here and learn to make low carb casseroles for a great weight loss.

Made in the USA
Monee, IL
20 September 2023

43064226R00024